Table Of Contents

Chapter 2. The Evolution of AI in Financial Markets 2
Chapter 3. Machine Learning Techniques for Option Trading 2
Chapter 4. Neural Networks in Option Trading 2
Chapter 5. Sentiment Analysis in Options Trading 2
Chapter 6. Predictive Analytics for Option Pricing 2
Chapter 7. Risk Management Strategies for Options Trading with AI 2
Chapter 8. Algorithmic Trading with AI 2
Chapter 9. High-Frequency Trading and AI 2
Chapter 10. Natural Language Processing in Options Trading 2
Chapter 11. Reinforcement Learning in Option Trading 2
Chapter 12. Genetic Algorithms in Option Trading 2
Chapter 13. Deep Learning Applications in Option Trading 2
Chapter 14. AI-Based Portfolio Optimization 2
Chapter 15. Market Microstructure and AI Trading 2
Chapter 16. Behavioral Finance and Options Trading 2
Chapter 17. Automated Trading Systems with AI 2
Chapter 18. Real-Time Data Analysis in Option Trading 2
Chapter 19. Machine Vision in Financial Markets 2
Chapter 20. AI-Powered Trading Platforms 2
Chapter 21. Cognitive Computing in Options Trading 2
Chapter 22. Big Data Analytics in Options Trading 2
Chapter 23. Robo-Advisors and Options Trading 2
Chapter 24. The Future of AI in Financial Markets 2
Chapter 25. Ethics and Regulation in AI Trading 2
Chapter 26. AI Assistants for Option Traders 2
Chapter 27. Quantitative Analysis in Options Trading 2
Chapter 28. AI Strategies for Volatility Trading 2
Chapter 29. Decision Support Systems for Options Trading 2
Chapter 30. AI and Hedge Fund Strategies 2
Chapter 31. Trading Psychology and AI 2
Chapter 32. Optimization Techniques for Options Trading 2
Chapter 33. AI and Market Liquidity 2
Chapter 34. Machine Learning Models for Options Pricing 2

Chapter 35. Algorithmic Trading Strategies with AI 2
Chapter 36. AI-Based Risk Assessment in Options Trading 2
Chapter 37. Natural Language Generation for Trading Reports 2
Chapter 38. AI and Market Anomalies 2
Chapter 39. Sentiment Analysis in Volatility Trading 2
Chapter 40. Machine Learning for Risk Prediction in Options Trading 2
Chapter 41. Quantum Computing and Options Trading 2
Chapter 42. AI-Driven Trading Algorithms 2
Chapter 43. Regulatory Compliance in AI Trading 2
Chapter 44. AI and Market Manipulation Detection 2
Chapter 45. Fintech Innovations in Options Trading 2
Chapter 46. AI and Market Forecasting 2
Chapter 47. AI Ethics and Bias in Trading 2
Chapter 48. AI-Based Market Surveillance 2
Chapter 49. Deep Reinforcement Learning in Options Trading 2
Chapter 50. The Intersection of AI and Behavioral Economics in Options Trading 2
Conclusion 2
Chapter 1. Introduction to AI and Option Trading 1

Chapter 1. Introduction to AI and Option Trading

Chapter 1: Introduction to AI and Option Trading

Welcome to the exciting world of AI-powered trading bots for executing options trades. In this subchapter, we will explore the fundamentals of AI and option trading, providing you with a solid foundation to begin your journey into the world of trading stocks and options. Whether you are a novice trader looking to learn the basics or an experienced investor seeking to leverage the power of AI technology in your trading strategies, this subchapter is designed to help you understand the key concepts and principles that drive success in the world of option trading.

First and foremost, it is important to understand what AI is and how it is revolutionizing the way we approach financial markets. Artificial intelligence, or AI, refers to the simulation of human intelligence processes by machines, particularly computer systems. In the context of option trading, AI can be used to analyze vast amounts of data, identify patterns and trends, and make informed decisions about when to buy or sell options. By harnessing the power of AI technology, traders can gain a competitive edge in the market and increase their chances of success.

When it comes to trading options, there are several key concepts that every trader should be familiar with. Options are financial derivatives that give traders the right, but not the obligation, to buy or sell an underlying asset at a specified price within a predetermined time frame. By trading options, investors can profit from market movements without actually owning the underlying asset. This flexibility and leverage make options an attractive investment vehicle for traders looking to maximize their returns and manage risk effectively.

One of the main advantages of using AI-powered trading bots for executing options trades is their ability to analyze market data and make decisions in real-time. These bots can scan the market for opportunities, execute trades automatically, and adjust their strategies based on changing market conditions. By leveraging AI technology, traders can eliminate human emotions from the trading process and make more objective, data-driven decisions. This can lead to more consistent results and improved performance over time.

In conclusion, mastering AI-powered trading bots for options requires a solid understanding of both AI technology and option trading principles. By combining the power of artificial intelligence with the flexibility of options trading, traders can create dynamic and profitable trading strategies that adapt to changing market conditions. Whether you are a beginner looking to learn the basics or an experienced investor seeking to enhance your trading skills, this subchapter will provide you with the knowledge and tools you need to succeed in the fast-paced world of AI and option trading.

Chapter 2. The Evolution of AI in Financial Markets

Chapter 2: The Evolution of AI in Financial Markets

In recent years, the use of artificial intelligence (AI) in financial markets has grown exponentially. This evolution has been driven by the increasing complexity of trading strategies and the need for faster and more accurate decision-making. AI-powered trading bots have become an indispensable tool for traders looking to optimize their performance in the fast-paced world of options trading.

The integration of AI technology in financial markets has revolutionized the way trading is conducted. These advanced algorithms are capable of analyzing vast amounts of data in real-time, identifying patterns and trends that human traders may not be able to detect. This gives traders a significant advantage in making informed decisions and executing trades with precision.

AI-powered trading bots have also proven to be highly efficient in executing options trades. These bots are programmed to automatically execute trades based on pre-defined parameters, reducing the risk of human error and ensuring that trades are executed at the optimal time and price. This level of automation allows traders to focus on developing and refining their trading strategies, rather than being bogged down by manual execution.

For those who are new to trading stocks and options, understanding the role of AI in financial markets is crucial. By learning how AI-powered trading bots operate and how they can be used to enhance trading performance, individuals can gain a competitive edge in the market. With the right knowledge and tools, even novice traders can leverage AI technology to improve their trading skills and achieve greater success in the world of options trading.

In conclusion, the evolution of AI in financial markets has paved the way for a new era of trading. By harnessing the power of AI-powered trading bots, traders can make more informed decisions, execute trades with precision, and ultimately achieve better results in the options market. By continuing to educate themselves on the capabilities of AI technology and how it can be applied to trading, individuals can position themselves for success in this dynamic and ever-changing industry.

Chapter 3. Machine Learning Techniques for Option Trading

Chapter 3: Machine Learning Techniques for Option Trading

In this chapter, we will delve into the exciting world of machine learning techniques for option trading. For those of you who are new to the world of trading stocks and options, machine learning is a powerful tool that can help you make more informed decisions when it comes to trading options. By using advanced algorithms and statistical models, machine learning can analyze large amounts of data to identify patterns and trends that can help you predict future market movements.

One of the key benefits of using machine learning techniques for option trading is the ability to automate the trading process. By using AI-powered trading bots, you can set up rules and parameters that will automatically execute trades based on the signals generated by the machine learning algorithms. This can help you take advantage of market opportunities in real-time without having to constantly monitor the market yourself.

Another advantage of using machine learning techniques for option trading is the ability to optimize your trading strategy. By analyzing historical data and market trends, machine learning algorithms can help you identify the most profitable trading strategies for your specific goals and risk tolerance. This can help you maximize your returns while minimizing your risk exposure.

When using machine learning techniques for option trading, it is important to keep in mind that these algorithms are not foolproof. While they can help you make more informed decisions, there is still a degree of uncertainty in the market that cannot be predicted with 100% accuracy. It is important to use machine learning techniques as a tool to supplement your trading strategy, rather than relying on them as the sole basis for your trading decisions.

In conclusion, machine learning techniques can be a powerful tool for those looking to enhance their options trading strategies. By using AI-powered trading bots and advanced algorithms, you can automate your trading process, optimize your trading strategy, and make more informed decisions in the market. However, it is important to remember that machine learning techniques are not infallible and should be used in conjunction with other analysis methods to create a well-rounded trading strategy.

Chapter 4. Neural Networks in Option Trading

In the world of trading options, advancements in artificial intelligence have revolutionized the way we approach decision-making and execution. Neural networks, a key component of AI technology, play a crucial role in analyzing market data and predicting future price movements. In this chapter, we will delve into how neural networks are used in option trading and how they can help you make more informed decisions when trading options.

Neural networks are a type of AI algorithm that mimics the way the human brain processes information. By analyzing vast amounts of historical market data, neural networks can identify patterns and trends that humans may overlook. This allows traders to make more accurate predictions about future price movements and make better-informed decisions when trading options.

One of the key advantages of using neural networks in option trading is their ability to adapt to changing market conditions. Unlike traditional trading algorithms that rely on fixed rules, neural networks can learn from new data and adjust their predictions accordingly. This flexibility allows traders to stay ahead of the curve and capitalize on emerging opportunities in the market.

Another benefit of using neural networks in option trading is their ability to handle complex data sets with ease. Whether you are analyzing stock prices, market trends, or economic indicators, neural networks can process large amounts of data quickly and efficiently. This allows traders to make faster and more accurate decisions when executing options trades.

Overall, neural networks are a powerful tool for traders looking to leverage AI technology in their option trading strategies. By harnessing the predictive capabilities of neural networks, traders can gain a competitive edge in the market and increase their chances of success. In the next chapter, we will explore how AI-powered trading bots can further enhance your options trading experience.

Chapter 5. Sentiment Analysis in Options Trading

In Chapter 5 of "Mastering AI-Powered Trading Bots for Options," we delve into the world of sentiment analysis in options trading. Sentiment analysis involves analyzing and interpreting the emotions and opinions expressed by traders in the market. By understanding the sentiment behind these trades, traders can make more informed decisions and potentially increase their chances of success in the options market.

For people eager to learn about trading stocks and options, sentiment analysis can provide valuable insights into market trends and potential opportunities. By utilizing AI-powered trading bots for executing options trades, traders can harness the power of sentiment analysis to stay ahead of the curve and make more strategic trading decisions.

One key benefit of sentiment analysis in options trading is the ability to gauge market sentiment in real-time. By analyzing social media posts, news articles, and other sources of information, traders can quickly assess market sentiment and adjust their trading strategies accordingly. This can be particularly useful in volatile market conditions where sentiment can change rapidly.

In addition to real-time market sentiment analysis, sentiment analysis can also help traders identify potential market trends and patterns. By analyzing historical data and sentiment indicators, traders can gain valuable insights into market behavior and make more informed decisions about when to enter or exit trades. This can be especially useful for traders looking to capitalize on short-term market movements in the options market.

Overall, sentiment analysis in options trading offers traders a powerful tool for making more informed trading decisions. By leveraging AI-powered trading bots and sentiment analysis tools, traders can gain a competitive edge in the market and increase their chances of success. Whether you are new to trading stocks and options or a seasoned trader, mastering sentiment analysis can help you navigate the complexities of the options market with confidence and precision.

Chapter 6. Predictive Analytics for Option Pricing

In Chapter 6, we delve into the fascinating world of predictive analytics for option pricing. For those who are new to trading stocks and options, predictive analytics involves using historical data and statistical algorithms to forecast future market trends. This powerful tool can help traders make more informed decisions when it comes to buying and selling options.

One of the key benefits of predictive analytics for option pricing is its ability to identify patterns and trends in the market that may not be immediately apparent to the naked eye. By analyzing large amounts of data, traders can gain valuable insights into how certain factors, such as interest rates, market volatility, and economic indicators, may impact the price of options. This information can then be used to make more accurate predictions about future market movements.

AI-powered trading bots play a crucial role in executing options trades based on predictive analytics. These bots are equipped with sophisticated algorithms that can quickly analyze market data and execute trades at lightning speed. By harnessing the power of AI, traders can automate their trading strategies and take advantage of profitable opportunities in the market.

For those looking to master AI-powered trading bots for executing options trades, it is essential to understand how predictive analytics can be used to enhance trading strategies. By incorporating predictive analytics into their decision-making process, traders can improve their chances of success in the market and maximize their profits. With the right tools and knowledge, anyone can learn to leverage the power of AI and predictive analytics to become a successful options trader.

In conclusion, Chapter 6 provides a comprehensive overview of how predictive analytics can be used to enhance option pricing and trading strategies. By learning how to leverage AI-powered trading bots and predictive analytics, traders can gain a competitive edge in the market and increase their chances of success. Whether you are a beginner or an experienced trader, mastering the art of predictive analytics for option pricing is a valuable skill that can help you achieve your trading goals.

Chapter 7. Risk Management Strategies for Options Trading with AI

In Chapter 7 of "Mastering AI-Powered Trading Bots for Options," we will delve into the essential topic of risk management strategies for options trading with AI. For those of you who are eager to learn about trading stocks and options, understanding how to effectively manage risk is crucial for long-term success in the market. With the integration of artificial intelligence (AI) technology in trading, the process of managing risk has become more sophisticated and efficient than ever before.

One of the key risk management strategies for options trading with AI is setting stop-loss orders. These orders automatically trigger a sell order when the price of an option reaches a certain level, limiting potential losses. By utilizing AI-powered trading bots to execute these stop-loss orders, traders can react quickly to market fluctuations and protect their investment portfolios from substantial losses. This proactive approach to risk management is essential for preserving capital and maximizing returns in the options market.

Another important risk management strategy for options trading with AI is diversification. By spreading your investments across a range of different options contracts and underlying assets, you can reduce the impact of any single trade on your overall portfolio. AI-powered trading bots can help you identify and execute diversified trading strategies, taking into account factors such as market trends, volatility, and correlation among assets. This strategic approach to risk management can help mitigate losses and optimize returns over time.

Furthermore, leveraging AI technology for options trading allows for the implementation of advanced risk assessment models. These models use historical data, market trends, and real-time information to analyze the potential risks associated with different options trades. By incorporating these risk assessment models into your trading strategy, you can make more informed decisions and minimize the likelihood of significant losses. AI-powered trading bots can execute these risk assessment models quickly and efficiently, providing you with valuable insights to guide your trading decisions.

In conclusion, mastering risk management strategies for options trading with AI is essential for anyone looking to succeed in the dynamic and competitive options market. By utilizing stop-loss orders, diversifying your portfolio, and leveraging advanced risk assessment models, you can minimize losses, protect your capital, and optimize returns. With the help of AI-powered trading bots, you can automate these risk management strategies and make data-driven decisions that enhance your trading performance. Stay tuned for the next chapter, where we will explore advanced technical analysis techniques for options trading with AI.

Chapter 8. Algorithmic Trading with AI

Algorithmic trading with AI has revolutionized the way trading stocks and options is done in the financial markets. For those who are just beginning to learn about trading stocks and options, understanding how AI can be used to make informed trading decisions is essential. In this chapter, we will explore the benefits of algorithmic trading with AI and how it can help you execute profitable options trades.

One of the key advantages of using AI in trading options is its ability to analyze vast amounts of data in real-time. AI-powered trading bots can quickly process market trends, news, and other relevant information to make accurate predictions about future price movements. This can give traders a competitive edge in the fast-paced world of options trading.

AI-powered trading bots are also able to execute trades with precision and speed that is unmatched by human traders. These bots can identify profitable opportunities and place trades within milliseconds, ensuring that you can take advantage of market fluctuations before they disappear. This can help you maximize your profits and minimize your losses in the volatile options market.

In addition to executing trades, AI-powered trading bots can also help you manage your risk more effectively. These bots can set stop-loss orders, monitor your portfolio for potential risks, and even adjust your trading strategy based on changing market conditions. By using AI to automate these processes, you can reduce the emotional bias that often leads to poor trading decisions.

Overall, algorithmic trading with AI offers a powerful tool for traders looking to optimize their options trading strategies. By leveraging the speed, accuracy, and risk management capabilities of AI-powered trading bots, you can increase your chances of success in the complex world of options trading. As you continue to learn and grow in your trading journey, consider incorporating AI into your trading toolkit to stay ahead of the curve.

Chapter 9. High-Frequency Trading and AI

In Chapter 9 of our book, we will delve into the fascinating world of high-frequency trading (HFT) and artificial intelligence (AI) in the context of trading options. This subchapter is designed for individuals who are eager to learn about the intersection of AI and trading options, as well as the potential benefits and risks associated with high-frequency trading.

High-frequency trading refers to the practice of executing a large number of trades at incredibly high speeds using sophisticated algorithms and powerful computing technology. This approach allows traders to capitalize on small price discrepancies in the market and generate profits in a matter of milliseconds. By leveraging AI-powered trading bots, traders can automate the process of executing options trades and react to market conditions with lightning speed.

One of the key advantages of using AI-powered trading bots for executing options trades is the ability to make split-second decisions based on complex market data and algorithms. These bots can analyze vast amounts of data, identify patterns, and execute trades with precision and efficiency. By incorporating AI into their trading strategies, individuals can potentially increase their chances of success and maximize their profits in the options market.

However, it is important to note that high-frequency trading and AI-powered trading bots also come with certain risks. The speed and complexity of these systems can lead to unintended consequences, such as market volatility and sudden price fluctuations. Additionally, there is a risk of technical glitches or malfunctions that could result in significant losses. It is crucial for traders to exercise caution and implement risk management strategies when using AI-powered trading bots for options trading.

In conclusion, Chapter 9 provides a comprehensive overview of high-frequency trading and AI in the context of options trading. By understanding the benefits and risks associated with these technologies, individuals can make informed decisions about incorporating AI-powered trading bots into their trading strategies. With the right knowledge and tools, traders can harness the power of AI to navigate the complex world of options trading and potentially achieve their financial goals.

Chapter 10. Natural Language Processing in Options Trading

In Chapter 10 of "Mastering AI-Powered Trading Bots for Options," we delve into the exciting world of Natural Language Processing (NLP) in options trading. NLP is a branch of artificial intelligence that focuses on the interaction between computers and human language. By incorporating NLP into options trading, traders can gain valuable insights from textual data sources such as news articles, social media posts, and analyst reports.

For people eager to learn about trading stocks and options, understanding how NLP can be applied in the field of options trading is essential. By analyzing large amounts of text data, NLP algorithms can help traders make more informed decisions by extracting key information and sentiment from the text. This can provide valuable insights into market trends, company performance, and potential trading opportunities.

One of the key benefits of using NLP in options trading is its ability to process vast amounts of textual data quickly and efficiently. By automating the analysis of news articles, social media posts, and other text sources, traders can stay ahead of market trends and make more informed decisions in real-time. This can give traders a competitive edge in the fast-paced world of options trading.

AI-powered trading bots can leverage NLP to execute options trades based on the insights gleaned from textual data sources. By incorporating NLP algorithms into trading bots, traders can automate the process of analyzing text data and making trading decisions. This can help traders save time and reduce the risk of human error, ultimately leading to more profitable trading strategies.

In conclusion, Chapter 10 of "Mastering AI-Powered Trading Bots for Options" emphasizes the critical role of Natural Language Processing (NLP) in optimizing options trading strategies. By leveraging NLP capabilities, traders can extract meaningful insights from diverse textual data sources, enabling them to make well-informed decisions amidst the dynamic and competitive landscape of options trading. For individuals intrigued by the intersection of artificial intelligence and options trading, comprehending the practical applications of NLP within this domain is paramount for achieving success and staying ahead in the market.t.

Chapter 11. Reinforcement Learning in Option Trading

In this chapter, we will delve into the exciting world of reinforcement learning in option trading. For those of you who are new to the concept, reinforcement learning is a type of machine learning algorithm that enables AI-powered trading bots to learn from their actions and make decisions based on maximizing rewards. This powerful tool has revolutionized the field of trading by allowing bots to continuously improve their strategies through trial and error.

When it comes to option trading, reinforcement learning can be particularly beneficial. Options are complex financial instruments that require sophisticated strategies to maximize profits and minimize risks.

By using reinforcement learning, trading bots can adapt to changing market conditions and optimize their decision-making process in real-time. This means that they can identify profitable opportunities and execute trades with precision and efficiency.

One of the key advantages of using reinforcement learning in option trading is its ability to handle large amounts of data and complex trading strategies. AI-powered trading bots can analyze vast amounts of historical and real-time data to identify trends and patterns that human traders may overlook. This allows them to make informed decisions and execute trades with confidence, even in volatile market conditions.

Furthermore, reinforcement learning allows trading bots to continuously learn and improve their performance over time. By receiving feedback on their actions and adjusting their strategies accordingly, these bots can become more effective and profitable traders. This iterative process of learning and optimization is what sets AI-powered trading bots apart from traditional trading methods.

In conclusion, reinforcement learning is a powerful tool that can significantly enhance the performance of AI-powered trading bots in option trading. By leveraging this technology, traders can improve their decision-making process, optimize their strategies, and ultimately increase their profits. As you continue to explore the world of AI and trading options, remember to embrace the potential of reinforcement learning to take your trading to the next level. It is crucial to stay updated on the latest advancements in AI technology and continuously adapt your trading strategies to stay ahead of the competition. By incorporating reinforcement learning into your trading approach, you can stay competitive in the market and achieve even greater success in your trading endeavors. Keep in mind that as technology continues to evolve, staying informed and open to new developments is key to maintaining a successful trading strategy. By staying proactive in your approach to utilizing AI tools, you can position yourself for continued growth and success in the dynamic world of option trading.

Chapter 12. Genetic Algorithms in Option Trading

In Chapter 12 of our book, "Mastering AI-Powered Trading Bots for Options," we dive into the fascinating world of genetic algorithms in option trading. For those who are new to the world of trading stocks and options, genetic algorithms offer a powerful tool for optimizing trading strategies and maximizing profits. By leveraging the power of artificial intelligence, traders can create sophisticated algorithms that can adapt and evolve over time to capitalize on market opportunities.

Genetic algorithms are a type of optimization technique inspired by the process of natural selection. By simulating the principles of evolution, genetic algorithms can help traders find the most effective trading strategies for their specific goals and risk tolerance. These algorithms work by generating a population of potential solutions, evaluating their performance, and selecting the best candidates to breed and produce the next generation of solutions.

One of the key benefits of using genetic algorithms in option trading is their ability to explore a wide range of potential solutions and quickly converge on the most optimal strategies. This can be particularly useful in the fast-paced world of options trading, where market conditions can change rapidly and traditional trading strategies may not always be effective. By harnessing the power of genetic algorithms, traders can adapt to changing market conditions and make more informed decisions about when to enter or exit trades.

In our book, we provide practical examples and step-by-step guides to help beginners understand how genetic algorithms can be applied to option trading. We cover topics such as creating fitness functions to evaluate trading strategies, selecting appropriate parameters for the genetic algorithm, and interpreting the results to make informed trading decisions. By following our guidance, readers can start to harness the power of genetic algorithms and AI-powered trading bots to enhance their trading performance and achieve their financial goals.

Whether you are a novice trader looking to learn more about the intersection of AI and trading options or an experienced investor seeking to leverage cutting-edge technology in your trading strategies, our book offers valuable insights and practical advice to help you succeed in the dynamic world of options trading. With genetic algorithms and AI-powered trading bots at your disposal, you can take your trading to the next level and unlock new opportunities for profit and growth.

Chapter 13. Deep Learning Applications in Option Trading

In Chapter 13 of our book "Mastering AI-Powered Trading Bots for Options," we delve into the exciting world of deep learning applications in option trading. For those who are just beginning to learn about trading stocks and options, this chapter will provide valuable insights into how artificial intelligence (AI) can revolutionize the way we approach financial markets.

Deep learning, a subset of AI, has gained popularity in recent years for its ability to analyze vast amounts of data and identify patterns that human traders may overlook. When applied to option trading, deep learning algorithms can help traders make more informed decisions by predicting market movements and identifying profitable opportunities.

One of the key benefits of using deep learning in option trading is its ability to adapt to changing market conditions. Traditional trading strategies may become obsolete as market dynamics shift, but deep learning algorithms can quickly adjust their predictions based on new information. This flexibility can give traders a competitive edge in fast-paced markets where timing is critical.

AI-powered trading bots have become increasingly popular for executing options trades due to their speed and accuracy. These bots can analyze market data in real-time, execute trades automatically, and even learn from past trades to improve performance over time. By incorporating deep learning algorithms into these bots, traders can leverage the power of AI to make more profitable trades with minimal human intervention.

As you continue your journey into the world of AI and trading options, exploring deep learning applications can help you gain a deeper understanding of how AI can be used to enhance your trading strategies. By staying informed about the latest developments in AI-powered trading bots and leveraging the power of deep learning algorithms, you can become a more successful and confident trader in today's complex and dynamic financial markets.

Chapter 14. AI-Based Portfolio Optimization

Chapter 14: AI-Based Portfolio Optimization

In this chapter, we will delve into the exciting world of AI-based portfolio optimization. For those of you who are just starting out in the world of trading stocks and options, this concept may seem daunting at first. However, with the help of AI-powered trading bots, you can streamline the process and make more informed decisions when it comes to managing your portfolio.

Portfolio optimization is the process of selecting the best mix of assets to achieve the desired level of return while minimizing risk. Traditionally, this has been done using complex mathematical models and statistical analysis. However, with the advent of artificial intelligence, traders now have access to powerful algorithms that can analyze vast amounts of data in real-time and provide actionable insights.

One of the key benefits of using AI-based portfolio optimization is the ability to adapt to changing market conditions. Unlike traditional models that rely on historical data, AI algorithms can quickly adjust to new information and make recommendations based on the most up-to-date market trends. This can help traders stay ahead of the curve and make more informed decisions when it comes to managing their investments.

Another advantage of AI-powered portfolio optimization is the ability to identify hidden patterns and correlations in the market. By analyzing large datasets, AI algorithms can uncover trends that may not be apparent to human traders. This can help investors uncover new opportunities and optimize their portfolios for maximum returns.

In conclusion, AI-based portfolio optimization is a powerful tool for traders looking to make more informed decisions when it comes to managing their investments. By leveraging the power of artificial intelligence, traders can gain a competitive edge in the market and maximize their returns. With the help of AI-powered trading bots, even novice traders can take advantage of these advanced technologies and improve their overall trading performance.

Chapter 15. Market Microstructure and AI Trading

Chapter 15: Market Microstructure and AI Trading

In this chapter, we will delve into the fascinating world of market microstructure and its relationship with AI trading. Market microstructure refers to the study of how markets operate and are structured, including the roles of market participants, trading venues, and the mechanisms through which trades are executed.

Understanding market microstructure is crucial for successful trading, as it provides insights into market dynamics and helps traders make more informed decisions.

AI trading has revolutionized the way trading is conducted, especially in the options market. By leveraging advanced algorithms and machine learning techniques, AI-powered trading bots can analyze vast amounts of data and execute trades with speed and precision that human traders simply cannot match. This has led to increased efficiency and profitability in options trading, making it an attractive option for both beginners and seasoned traders alike.

One key aspect of market microstructure that AI trading bots take advantage of is order flow. Order flow refers to the flow of buy and sell orders in the market, which can provide valuable information about market sentiment and potential price movements. AI algorithms can analyze order flow data in real-time and make split-second decisions on when to enter or exit trades, giving traders a competitive edge in the market.

Another important concept in market microstructure is liquidity. Liquidity refers to the ease with which an asset can be bought or sold without causing significant price movements. AI trading bots are designed to optimize trade execution by taking into account liquidity conditions in the market, ensuring that trades are executed efficiently and at the best possible prices. This can help traders minimize slippage and maximize profits in their options trading strategies.

In conclusion, market microstructure plays a critical role in AI-powered trading bots for executing options trades. By understanding how markets operate and leveraging AI technology, traders can gain a competitive advantage and improve their trading performance. Whether you are just starting out in trading stocks and options or are looking to enhance your existing trading strategies, mastering the relationship between market microstructure and AI trading is essential for success in today's fast-paced and dynamic markets.

Chapter 16. Behavioral Finance and Options Trading

In Chapter 16 of our book, we delve into the fascinating world of behavioral finance and its implications for options trading. Understanding the psychology behind trading decisions can give traders a competitive edge in the market, especially when combined with the power of AI technology. By learning how human emotions and biases can impact trading outcomes, traders can make more informed decisions and improve their overall success rate.

Behavioral finance is a field that combines psychology and economics to study how individuals make financial decisions. This discipline recognizes that humans are not always rational beings and that emotions can play a significant role in shaping our choices. By understanding common biases such as loss aversion, overconfidence, and herd mentality, traders can better navigate the complexities of the market and avoid falling prey to common pitfalls.

When it comes to options trading, behavioral finance can provide valuable insights into market trends and patterns. By analyzing how other traders react to news events or changes in market conditions, traders can anticipate potential price movements and adjust their strategies accordingly. This can be especially useful when using AI-powered trading bots, which can quickly analyze vast amounts of data and execute trades at lightning speed.

AI-powered trading bots are revolutionizing the world of options trading by automating the process and removing human error from the equation. These sophisticated algorithms can analyze market data in real-time, identify profitable opportunities, and execute trades with precision. By combining the power of AI technology with the insights of behavioral finance, traders can create a winning strategy that maximizes their chances of success in the market.

In conclusion, Chapter 16 explores the intersection of behavioral finance and options trading, offering valuable insights for traders looking to improve their performance. By understanding the psychological factors that influence trading decisions and leveraging the power of AI technology, traders can gain a competitive edge in the market and achieve greater success. Whether you are a novice trader or an experienced investor, mastering the principles of behavioral finance and AI-powered trading bots can help you navigate the complexities of the market and make more informed decisions.

Chapter 17. Automated Trading Systems with AI

Chapter 17: Automated Trading Systems with AI

In this chapter, we will delve into the fascinating world of Automated Trading Systems with AI. Automated trading systems are revolutionizing the way traders approach the stock and options markets. By incorporating artificial intelligence into these systems, traders can execute trades with greater speed, accuracy, and efficiency than ever before. This subchapter is designed for people eager to learn about trading stocks and options, particularly those interested in the intersection of AI and trading options.

AI-powered trading bots are becoming increasingly popular in the financial markets due to their ability to analyze vast amounts of data and make split-second trading decisions. These bots can execute trades at lightning speed, taking advantage of market opportunities that human traders may miss. By incorporating AI into trading systems, traders can automate their strategies and minimize emotional decision-making, leading to more consistent and profitable trading results.

One of the key benefits of using AI-powered trading bots for executing options trades is their ability to adapt to changing market conditions. These bots can analyze market trends, news events, and other factors in real-time, adjusting their trading strategies accordingly. This flexibility allows traders to capitalize on opportunities and minimize losses in volatile market conditions.

Another advantage of automated trading systems with AI is the ability to backtest trading strategies. By simulating trades using historical data, traders can evaluate the performance of their strategies and make adjustments as needed. This allows traders to fine-tune their strategies and optimize their trading bot's performance before risking real capital in the market.

In conclusion, Automated Trading Systems with AI are revolutionizing the way traders approach the stock and options markets. By incorporating artificial intelligence into trading systems, traders can execute trades with greater speed, accuracy, and efficiency. For those eager to learn about trading stocks and options, exploring the world of AI-powered trading bots for executing options trades can provide valuable insights and opportunities for profitable trading.

Chapter 18. Real-Time Data Analysis in Option Trading

In Chapter 18 of our book, we will delve into the exciting world of real-time data analysis in option trading. For those of you who are just beginning to learn about trading stocks and options, understanding how to analyze real-time data is crucial for making informed trading decisions. With the rise of AI-powered trading bots, the ability to analyze data in real-time has become more accessible than ever before.

Real-time data analysis involves the continuous monitoring and interpretation of market data as it happens. This includes tracking price movements, volume changes, and other key indicators that can help traders identify trends and patterns in the market. By utilizing AI-powered trading bots, traders can automate the process of analyzing real-time data, allowing for faster decision-making and more efficient trades.

One of the key benefits of real-time data analysis in option trading is the ability to react quickly to changing market conditions. By analyzing data in real-time, traders can identify potential opportunities or risks and make timely adjustments to their trading strategies. This can help traders maximize profits and minimize losses in a fast-paced market environment.

AI-powered trading bots play a crucial role in real-time data analysis by utilizing advanced algorithms to process and interpret market data in a fraction of the time it would take a human trader. These bots can analyze vast amounts of data simultaneously, allowing for more accurate and timely trading decisions. By incorporating AI-powered trading bots into your trading strategy, you can gain a competitive edge in the options market.

In conclusion, mastering real-time data analysis in option trading is essential for anyone looking to succeed in the world of trading stocks and options. By leveraging AI-powered trading bots to analyze data in real-time, traders can make more informed decisions, react quickly to market changes, and ultimately improve their trading performance. So, whether you are a beginner or an experienced trader, understanding how to analyze real-time data is a valuable skill that can help you achieve success in the world of options trading. It is important to continuously stay updated on the latest market trends, utilize advanced analytics tools, and adapt your trading strategies accordingly to stay ahead of the competition.

Investing time and effort into honing your data analysis skills can give you a competitive edge in the fast-paced world of options trading, allowing you to maximize your profits and minimize risks in the ever-changing market environment.

Chapter 19. Machine Vision in Financial Markets

Chapter 19: Machine Vision in Financial Markets

In the ever-evolving world of financial markets, the integration of machine vision technology has revolutionized the way traders analyze data and make decisions. Machine vision, a subset of artificial intelligence, allows trading bots to interpret and understand visual information from charts, graphs, and other financial data sources. This advanced technology enables traders to identify patterns, trends, and anomalies that may not be apparent to the human eye, providing them with a competitive edge in the market.

For people eager to learn about trading stocks and options, understanding the role of machine vision in financial markets is essential. By harnessing the power of AI and machine vision, traders can automate the analysis of vast amounts of data, allowing them to make more informed decisions and execute trades with greater precision. With the help of AI-powered trading bots, traders can leverage machine vision technology to optimize their trading strategies and improve their overall performance in the options market.

One of the key benefits of using machine vision in financial markets is its ability to quickly analyze and interpret complex data sets in real-time. This enables traders to react swiftly to market changes and make decisions based on accurate and up-to-date information. By incorporating machine vision technology into their trading bots, traders can gain a deeper understanding of market trends and dynamics, allowing them to capitalize on opportunities and mitigate risks effectively.

Furthermore, machine vision technology can help traders identify patterns and correlations that may not be immediately apparent, enabling them to make more informed trading decisions. By using AI-powered trading bots equipped with machine vision capabilities, traders can automate the process of analyzing charts, graphs, and other visual data sources, saving valuable time and resources. This allows traders to focus on developing and implementing effective trading strategies, rather than getting bogged down in manual data analysis.

In conclusion, the integration of machine vision technology in financial markets has opened up a world of possibilities for traders looking to enhance their trading capabilities. By leveraging AI-powered trading bots equipped with machine vision capabilities, traders can gain a competitive edge in the options market by making more informed decisions and executing trades with greater precision. For those eager to learn about trading stocks and options, understanding the role of machine vision in financial markets is crucial for success in today's fast-paced and dynamic trading environment.

Chapter 20. AI-Powered Trading Platforms

Chapter 20: AI-Powered Trading Platforms

In this chapter, we will delve into the exciting world of AI-powered trading platforms. These platforms utilize artificial intelligence to analyze market trends, execute trades, and optimize trading strategies. For individuals looking to enhance their trading skills and capitalize on the fast-paced world of stock and options trading, AI-powered platforms offer a powerful tool to stay ahead of the game.

AI-powered trading platforms leverage advanced algorithms to process vast amounts of data in real-time. By analyzing historical market data, current trends, and news events, these platforms can identify profitable trading opportunities with speed and accuracy that far surpass human capabilities. This allows traders to make informed decisions and execute trades with precision, even in volatile market conditions.

One of the key advantages of AI-powered trading platforms is their ability to adapt and learn from market conditions. Through machine learning algorithms, these platforms can continuously improve their trading strategies based on past performance and market feedback. This dynamic approach enables traders to stay agile and adjust their strategies in response to changing market conditions, maximizing their chances of success in the highly competitive world of trading options.

For individuals new to trading stocks and options, AI-powered trading platforms offer a valuable resource to learn and practice trading strategies. These platforms provide users with access to a wealth of educational resources, including tutorials, webinars, and demo accounts. By leveraging the power of AI, traders can simulate trades, test strategies, and gain hands-on experience in a risk-free environment before committing real capital to the market.

In conclusion, AI-powered trading platforms are revolutionizing the way traders approach stock and options trading. By harnessing the power of artificial intelligence, traders can gain a competitive edge, optimize their trading strategies, and make informed decisions in real-time. For individuals eager to learn and master the art of trading options, AI-powered platforms offer a valuable tool to enhance their skills and achieve success in the dynamic world of financial markets.

Chapter 21. Cognitive Computing in Options Trading

In this chapter, we will delve into the exciting world of cognitive computing in options trading. Cognitive computing refers to the use of computer algorithms that mimic the way the human brain processes information. By incorporating cognitive computing into options trading, traders can make more informed decisions and potentially increase their profits.

One of the key benefits of using cognitive computing in options trading is the ability to analyze vast amounts of data in a fraction of the time it would take a human trader. Cognitive computing algorithms can process news articles, social media posts, market data, and other relevant information to identify potential trading opportunities. This can give traders a competitive edge in the fast-paced world of options trading.

Another advantage of cognitive computing in options trading is the ability to adapt to changing market conditions. Cognitive computing algorithms can learn from past trading experiences and continuously improve their performance over time. This adaptability is crucial in options trading, where market conditions can change rapidly and unpredictably.

Furthermore, cognitive computing can help traders identify patterns and trends in the options market that may not be immediately apparent to human traders. By analyzing historical data and identifying correlations between different variables, cognitive computing algorithms can uncover hidden opportunities for profitable trades.

Overall, incorporating cognitive computing into options trading can help traders make more informed decisions, adapt to changing market conditions, and identify profitable trading opportunities that may not be obvious to human traders. By leveraging the power of cognitive computing, traders can potentially increase their profits and achieve greater success in the world of options trading. This advanced technology enables traders to analyze vast amounts of data quickly and accurately, leading to more strategic decision-making and a competitive edge in the market. Additionally, cognitive computing can provide valuable insights and predictions based on historical trends and real-time market data, giving traders a more comprehensive understanding of market dynamics and potential risks. Ultimately, embracing cognitive computing in options trading can revolutionize the way traders approach the market, ultimately leading to improved performance and increased profitability.

Chapter 22. Big Data Analytics in Options Trading

In the world of options trading, the use of big data analytics has revolutionized the way traders make decisions and execute trades. By leveraging vast amounts of data from various sources, traders can gain valuable insights into market trends, opportunities, and risks. This chapter will explore how big data analytics can be used to enhance your options trading strategies and maximize your profits.

One of the key benefits of using big data analytics in options trading is the ability to identify patterns and trends that may not be apparent to the naked eye. By analyzing historical data, market news, social media sentiment, and other relevant information, traders can uncover hidden opportunities and make more informed decisions. This can help you stay ahead of the curve and capitalize on emerging trends before they become mainstream.

Another advantage of using big data analytics in options trading is the ability to predict market movements with greater accuracy. By analyzing large volumes of data in real-time, traders can identify potential price movements and adjust their strategies accordingly. This can help you minimize risk and maximize returns by taking advantage of market fluctuations and opportunities as they arise.

Furthermore, big data analytics can help traders optimize their trading strategies by providing insights into market behavior, volatility, and risk factors. By analyzing data on a granular level, traders can fine-tune their strategies to better align with their goals and risk tolerance. This can help you make more confident and profitable trading decisions, even in volatile market conditions.

In conclusion, big data analytics plays a crucial role in options trading by providing traders with valuable insights, predictive capabilities, and optimization opportunities. By leveraging the power of big data, traders can enhance their decision-making processes, identify profitable opportunities, and mitigate risks. As you continue to learn and master the art of trading options, consider incorporating big data analytics into your strategy to stay ahead of the competition and achieve greater success in the market.

Chapter 23. Robo-Advisors and Options Trading

In Chapter 23 of our book "Mastering AI-Powered Trading Bots for Options," we delve into the exciting world of robo-advisors and options trading. For those of you who are new to the concept, robo-advisors are automated investment platforms that use algorithms to make investment decisions on your behalf. In the realm of options trading, robo-advisors can be incredibly helpful in executing trades quickly and efficiently.

For people eager to learn about trading stocks and options, understanding the role of AI in trading options is essential. AI-powered trading bots have revolutionized the way options trades are executed, offering speed and accuracy that human traders simply cannot match. By harnessing the power of AI, traders can make better decisions and maximize their profits in the fast-paced world of options trading.

One of the key benefits of using robo-advisors in options trading is their ability to analyze vast amounts of data in real-time. These AI-powered algorithms can quickly assess market trends, identify potential trading opportunities, and execute trades at lightning speed. This level of efficiency can give traders a significant edge in the highly competitive options market.

Another advantage of using robo-advisors in options trading is the elimination of human emotions from the trading process. Emotions such as fear and greed can often cloud judgment and lead to poor decision-making. By relying on AI-powered trading bots, traders can remove these emotional biases and make decisions based on data and logic, leading to more consistent and profitable trading outcomes.

In conclusion, Chapter 23 provides a detailed and thorough examination of the significant role that robo-advisors and AI-powered trading bots play in the realm of options trading. For individuals who are enthusiastic about delving deeper into the world of trading stocks and options, gaining a solid understanding of the advantages that AI can offer in trading is crucial for making well-informed investment decisions and attaining heightened success in the options market. By embracing the capabilities of AI technology, you can elevate your trading strategies and propel your trading endeavors to new heights with the assistance of robo-advisors in executing options trades effectively and efficiently.

Chapter 24. The Future of AI in Financial Markets

In Chapter 24, we will delve into the exciting topic of the future of AI in financial markets. As technology continues to advance at a rapid pace, artificial intelligence (AI) is revolutionizing the way trading stocks and options are conducted. For those eager to learn about trading stocks and options, understanding the role of AI in financial markets is crucial for success in today's fast-paced trading environment.

AI and trading options go hand in hand, as AI-powered trading bots are increasingly being used to execute complex options trades with speed and precision. These bots are equipped with sophisticated algorithms that analyze market data, identify trading opportunities, and execute trades automatically based on pre-defined parameters. By harnessing the power of AI, traders can take advantage of market inefficiencies and make more informed trading decisions.

One of the key advantages of AI-powered trading bots for executing options trades is their ability to process vast amounts of data in real time. This allows traders to react quickly to market changes and capitalize on opportunities before they disappear. With AI, traders can automate their trading strategies and minimize the emotional biases that often lead to costly trading mistakes.

As AI technology continues to evolve, the future of AI in financial markets looks promising. AI-powered trading bots will become even more advanced, with the ability to learn from past trades and improve their performance over time. This will give traders a competitive edge in the market and help them achieve consistent profits in their trading endeavors.

In conclusion, mastering AI-powered trading bots for options is essential for anyone looking to succeed in the world of trading stocks and options. By understanding the role of AI in financial markets and leveraging the power of AI-powered trading bots, traders can enhance their trading strategies, minimize risks, and achieve greater success in their trading endeavors. The future of AI in financial markets holds immense potential for those willing to embrace this cutting-edge technology and harness its power for profitable trading.

Chapter 25. Ethics and Regulation in AI Trading

In Chapter 25, we delve into the crucial topic of ethics and regulation in AI trading. As individuals venturing into the world of trading stocks and options, it is essential to understand the ethical considerations and regulatory frameworks that govern the use of artificial intelligence in trading. By mastering these concepts, you can navigate the complex landscape of AI-powered trading bots with confidence and integrity.

Ethics play a significant role in AI trading, as the use of algorithms and machine learning can present ethical dilemmas. It is crucial to consider the potential impact of AI trading on market stability, fairness, and transparency. As a trader, it is your responsibility to ensure that your AI-powered trading bots adhere to ethical standards and do not engage in manipulative or deceptive practices. By understanding the ethical implications of AI trading, you can make informed decisions that align with your values and principles.

Regulation is another critical aspect of AI trading that traders must be familiar with. Regulatory bodies such as the Securities and Exchange Commission (SEC) play a vital role in overseeing the use of AI in trading and ensuring compliance with laws and regulations. As a trader, it is essential to stay informed about the latest regulatory developments and comply with all relevant laws and guidelines. By following regulatory requirements, you can protect yourself from legal risks and ensure the integrity of your trading activities.

When using AI-powered trading bots for executing options trades, it is essential to prioritize transparency and accountability. Make sure that you understand how your bots operate, including the algorithms they use and the data they rely on. By maintaining transparency, you can build trust with your clients and stakeholders and demonstrate your commitment to ethical trading practices. Additionally, establishing accountability mechanisms can help you track the performance of your bots and take corrective action if necessary.

In conclusion, mastering the concepts of ethics and regulation in AI trading is essential for anyone seeking to excel in the world of options trading. By understanding the ethical considerations and regulatory frameworks that govern AI trading, you can make informed decisions, mitigate risks, and build a reputation as a responsible and ethical trader. As you continue your journey in AI-powered trading bots for executing options trades, remember to prioritize transparency, accountability, and ethical conduct to ensure long-term success and sustainability in the market.

Chapter 26. AI Assistants for Option Traders

Chapter 26: AI Assistants for Option Traders

In the world of trading options, having the right tools at your disposal can make all the difference in your success. One of the most powerful tools available to option traders today is the use of AI assistants. These sophisticated programs are designed to analyze market data, identify trends, and execute trades on your behalf with speed and precision.

AI-powered trading bots have revolutionized the way that options traders operate. By utilizing advanced algorithms and machine learning techniques, these bots can process vast amounts of data in real-time to make informed decisions about when to buy or sell options. This level of automation can help traders stay ahead of market movements and capitalize on opportunities that may be missed by human traders.

For those who are just beginning to learn about trading stocks and options, AI assistants can be particularly valuable. These programs can help to simplify the trading process and provide valuable insights into market dynamics. By using an AI assistant, novice traders can gain a deeper understanding of how options trading works and develop their skills more quickly.

AI assistants for option traders are also beneficial for more experienced traders who are looking to enhance their trading strategies. These bots can help to identify new trading opportunities, manage risk more effectively, and optimize trading performance. By incorporating AI-powered tools into their workflows, seasoned traders can take their trading to the next level and achieve greater success in the options market.

In conclusion, AI assistants for option traders represent a powerful tool for anyone looking to improve their trading skills and achieve better results in the options market. By leveraging the capabilities of these sophisticated programs, traders can gain a competitive edge, make more informed decisions, and maximize their trading profits. Whether you are a beginner or an experienced trader, incorporating AI assistants into your trading arsenal can help you to achieve your financial goals and become a more successful options trader.

Chapter 27. Quantitative Analysis in Options Trading

In the world of stock trading and options, quantitative analysis plays a crucial role in making informed decisions and maximizing profits. By utilizing mathematical and statistical models, traders can analyze market data, identify patterns, and predict future price movements with a high degree of accuracy. This subchapter will delve into the importance of quantitative analysis in options trading and how it can be effectively used to enhance your trading strategies.

One of the key benefits of quantitative analysis in options trading is its ability to provide traders with a systematic approach to decision-making. By using algorithms and mathematical models, traders can eliminate emotions from their trading process and rely on data-driven insights to make informed choices. This can help reduce the impact of human bias and improve the overall performance of your trading portfolio.

Another advantage of quantitative analysis in options trading is its ability to identify trading opportunities that may not be immediately apparent to the naked eye. By analyzing historical market data, traders can uncover patterns and trends that can be exploited for profit. This can give traders a competitive edge in the market and help them stay ahead of the curve when it comes to executing successful trades.

In the realm of AI and trading options, quantitative analysis is essential for developing AI-powered trading bots that can execute trades autonomously based on predefined criteria. These bots can analyze vast amounts of market data in real-time, identify trading opportunities, and execute trades at lightning speed. By leveraging the power of AI, traders can automate their trading strategies and take advantage of market opportunities 24/7.

In conclusion, mastering quantitative analysis in options trading is essential for anyone looking to succeed in the fast-paced world of stock trading and options. By understanding the principles of quantitative analysis, utilizing mathematical models and algorithms, and leveraging the power of AI-powered trading bots, traders can enhance their trading strategies, make informed decisions, and maximize their profits in the market. So, start learning and practicing quantitative analysis today to take your trading game to the next level.

Chapter 28. AI Strategies for Volatility Trading

Chapter 28: AI Strategies for Volatility Trading

In the world of trading stocks and options, volatility can be a double-edged sword. On one hand, it can present lucrative opportunities for profit, but on the other hand, it can also lead to significant losses if not managed properly. This is where AI-powered trading bots come into play, offering sophisticated strategies for navigating the ever-changing landscape of volatility in the market.

One key strategy for trading options in volatile markets is to use AI algorithms to identify patterns and trends that can help predict price movements. By analyzing historical data and market indicators, these bots can make informed decisions about when to buy or sell options to take advantage of volatility. This can help traders maximize profits while minimizing risk in uncertain market conditions.

Another important aspect of volatility trading is risk management. AI-powered trading bots can help traders set stop-loss orders and other risk management tools to protect their investments in the face of sudden market swings. By using advanced algorithms to monitor market conditions in real-time, these bots can react quickly to changes and help traders avoid catastrophic losses.

Furthermore, AI strategies for volatility trading can also help traders diversify their portfolios and spread risk across different assets. By using machine learning algorithms to optimize portfolio allocation based on market conditions, traders can reduce their exposure to any single asset or sector and increase their chances of long-term success in the market.

In conclusion, mastering AI-powered trading bots for options can be a valuable tool for those looking to navigate the complexities of volatility trading. By leveraging advanced algorithms and machine learning techniques, traders can gain a competitive edge in the market and increase their chances of success. With the right strategies and risk management tools in place, traders can capitalize on the opportunities presented by volatility while protecting their investments from potential losses.

Chapter 29. Decision Support Systems for Options Trading

Chapter 29: Decision Support Systems for Options Trading

In the fast-paced world of options trading, having the right tools at your disposal can make all the difference between success and failure. One such tool that has revolutionized the way traders approach the market is Decision Support Systems (DSS). These systems use artificial intelligence (AI) algorithms to analyze market data and provide valuable insights into potential trading opportunities.

For those who are new to trading stocks and options, understanding how DSS can enhance your trading strategy is crucial. By leveraging AI-powered technology, traders can make more informed decisions and increase their chances of profitability. DSS can help traders identify patterns in the market, predict price movements, and even automate the execution of trades.

When it comes to trading options, having a reliable DSS in place can give traders a competitive edge. By using historical data, technical indicators, and market trends, these systems can help traders identify potential entry and exit points for their trades. This can significantly reduce the guesswork involved in trading options and increase the likelihood of making profitable decisions.

One of the key benefits of using DSS for options trading is the ability to backtest trading strategies. By simulating trades based on historical data, traders can see how their strategies would have performed in the past. This allows traders to fine-tune their strategies and make adjustments before risking real capital in the market.

In conclusion, for those looking to master AI-powered trading bots for executing options trades, incorporating a Decision Support System into your trading arsenal is essential. By harnessing the power of AI technology, traders can gain valuable insights, automate trading decisions, and ultimately increase their chances of success in the options market. So, whether you are a beginner or an experienced trader, embracing DSS can help take your trading to the next level.

Chapter 30. AI and Hedge Fund Strategies

In today's fast-paced world of trading stocks and options, artificial intelligence (AI) has become an invaluable tool for hedge funds and individual traders alike. AI-powered trading bots have revolutionized the way trades are executed, providing faster decision-making and more accurate predictions than ever before. In this chapter, we will explore how AI is reshaping hedge fund strategies and how you can leverage this technology to improve your own trading practices.

Hedge funds are increasingly turning to AI-powered trading bots to gain a competitive edge in the market. These bots use complex algorithms to analyze massive amounts of data and make split-second decisions on when to buy or sell securities. By harnessing the power of AI, hedge funds can execute trades more efficiently and with greater precision, leading to higher returns for their investors.

For individuals who are new to trading stocks and options, AI-powered trading bots offer a unique opportunity to level the playing field with professional traders. By utilizing AI algorithms, you can access real-time market data and make informed decisions on when to enter or exit trades. This can help you minimize risk and maximize profits, even if you have limited experience in the world of trading.

One of the key benefits of using AI-powered trading bots for executing options trades is the ability to automate repetitive tasks and streamline your trading process. These bots can analyze market trends, identify trading opportunities, and execute trades on your behalf, saving you time and effort. By letting AI do the heavy lifting, you can focus on developing your trading strategy and honing your skills as a trader.

In conclusion, AI has the potential to revolutionize the way we trade stocks and options, offering unprecedented opportunities for both hedge funds and individual traders. By understanding how AI-powered trading bots work and how they can benefit your trading practices, you can stay ahead of the curve and maximize your profits in the market. Whether you are a seasoned investor or just starting out, embracing AI technology can help you achieve your financial goals and become a successful trader in today's competitive market.

Chapter 31. Trading Psychology and AI

Chapter 31: Trading Psychology and AI

In the world of trading stocks and options, the intersection of trading psychology and artificial intelligence (AI) is crucial for success. Understanding how human emotions can impact trading decisions, as well as how AI-powered trading bots can help mitigate these emotions, is essential for those looking to master the art of trading options.

Trading psychology plays a significant role in the success of a trader. Emotions such as fear, greed, and overconfidence can cloud judgment and lead to irrational trading decisions. By recognizing and understanding these emotions, traders can develop strategies to manage them effectively. AI-powered trading bots can assist in this process by executing trades based on pre-defined rules and parameters, eliminating the potential for emotional decision-making.

AI technology has revolutionized the way we trade options. By utilizing machine learning algorithms and data analysis, AI-powered trading bots can analyze market trends and make informed decisions in real-time. This allows traders to execute trades quickly and efficiently, taking advantage of market opportunities as they arise.

When combining trading psychology with AI technology, traders can create a powerful strategy for success. By leveraging the strengths of both human intuition and AI precision, traders can make informed decisions while minimizing the impact of emotional biases. This hybrid approach can lead to more consistent and profitable trading outcomes.

In conclusion, mastering the relationship between trading psychology and AI is essential for those looking to excel in the world of trading options. By understanding the impact of emotions on trading decisions and leveraging the power of AI technology, traders can develop a winning strategy that maximizes profits and minimizes risks. With dedication and practice, anyone can learn to harness the power of AI-powered trading bots for executing options trades successfully.

Chapter 32. Optimization Techniques for Options Trading

Chapter 32: Optimization Techniques for Options Trading

In this subchapter, we will delve into the various optimization techniques that can be applied to options trading, specifically focusing on AI-powered trading bots. For individuals who are eager to learn about trading stocks and options, understanding how to optimize your trading strategies can make a significant difference in your success as a trader.

One important optimization technique for options trading is the use of machine learning algorithms to analyze market data and identify potential trading opportunities. By leveraging AI technology, traders can quickly and accurately identify patterns and trends in the market that may not be readily apparent to human traders. This can help traders make more informed decisions and execute profitable trades with greater efficiency.

Another key optimization technique is backtesting, which involves testing a trading strategy using historical market data to evaluate its performance. By backtesting their strategies, traders can identify areas for improvement and make adjustments to enhance their overall trading performance. AI-powered trading bots can automate the backtesting process, allowing traders to quickly test multiple strategies and optimize their trading approach.

Risk management is also a critical aspect of options trading that can be optimized using AI technology. By using machine learning algorithms to analyze market data and assess risk factors, traders can develop more effective risk management strategies to protect their capital and minimize losses. AI-powered trading bots can help traders automate their risk management processes, ensuring that they adhere to their predetermined risk tolerance levels.

In conclusion, mastering optimization techniques for options trading is essential for individuals looking to enhance their trading skills and achieve success in the market. By leveraging AI-powered trading bots and machine learning algorithms, traders can gain a competitive edge in the market and make more informed trading decisions. By continuously refining and optimizing their trading strategies, traders can increase their profitability and achieve their financial goals in the world of options trading.

Chapter 33. AI and Market Liquidity

Chapter 33: AI and Market Liquidity

In the world of trading stocks and options, market liquidity plays a crucial role in determining the ease of buying or selling assets. Liquidity refers to the ability of an asset to be quickly bought or sold without significantly affecting its price. In this chapter, we will explore how artificial intelligence (AI) is revolutionizing market liquidity and enhancing the trading experience for investors.

AI-powered trading bots are becoming increasingly popular in the world of options trading. These bots use advanced algorithms and machine learning techniques to analyze market data, identify trading opportunities, and execute trades with precision and speed. By leveraging AI technology, traders can access real-time market information and make informed decisions to maximize their returns.

One of the key benefits of using AI-powered trading bots for executing options trades is their ability to improve market liquidity. These bots are programmed to continuously monitor market conditions and execute trades at the most optimal times, thereby increasing liquidity in the market. This improved liquidity not only benefits individual traders by reducing the impact of their trades on asset prices but also contributes to a more efficient and stable market overall.

Moreover, AI-powered trading bots can help traders navigate complex trading environments and identify profitable opportunities that may be overlooked by human traders. By analyzing vast amounts of historical and real-time data, these bots can detect patterns and trends that human traders may miss, allowing them to make more informed trading decisions. As a result, traders can enhance their trading strategies and improve their overall performance in the options market.

In conclusion, AI technology is revolutionizing the way traders navigate market liquidity and carry out options trades. Through the utilization of AI-powered trading bots, traders can effectively tap into real-time market data, bolster liquidity, and refine their trading tactics. As traders delve deeper into the realm of stock and options trading, it is prudent to explore the integration of AI technology into their trading toolkit in order to remain at the forefront of market trends and optimize their opportunities for success in the ever-evolving market landscape. The implementation of AI technology not only enhances efficiency but also provides traders with a competitive edge in the fast-paced and dynamic world of financial markets. By harnessing the power of AI, traders can make more informed decisions, mitigate risks, and capitalize on emerging opportunities with greater precision and agility. Embracing AI technology is essential for traders looking to stay ahead of the curve and adapt to the rapidly changing market conditions, ultimately maximizing their potential for long-term success and profitability.

Chapter 34. Machine Learning Models for Options Pricing

In Chapter 34 of our book "Mastering AI-Powered Trading Bots for Options," we delve into the fascinating world of machine learning models for options pricing. For those of you who are eager to learn more about trading stocks and options, this subchapter is designed to provide you with a comprehensive understanding of how AI can be used to predict the price of options with greater accuracy.

Machine learning models have revolutionized the field of options pricing by allowing traders to analyze vast amounts of data and make more informed decisions. These models use complex algorithms to identify patterns and trends in market data, helping traders to predict the future price of options with a higher degree of accuracy.

One of the key advantages of using machine learning models for options pricing is their ability to adapt to changing market conditions. Unlike traditional pricing models, which rely on static assumptions, machine learning models can continuously learn from new data and adjust their predictions accordingly. This flexibility allows traders to stay ahead of the curve and make more profitable trades.

In this subchapter, we will explore some of the most commonly used machine learning models for options pricing, including neural networks, support vector machines, and random forests. We will explain how these models work, their strengths and weaknesses, and how they can be applied to real-world trading scenarios.

By the end of this subchapter, you will have a solid understanding of how machine learning models can be used to price options more accurately and effectively. Whether you are new to trading stocks and options or an experienced trader looking to enhance your skills, mastering AI-powered trading bots for executing options trades will give you the competitive edge you need to succeed in today's fast-paced market.

Chapter 35. Algorithmic Trading Strategies with AI

In this chapter, we will delve into the world of algorithmic trading strategies with AI, a powerful tool that can help you stay ahead in the fast-paced world of stock and options trading. As technology continues to advance, it has become increasingly important for traders to leverage artificial intelligence to make informed decisions and execute trades in a timely manner.

Algorithmic trading strategies with AI involve using complex mathematical algorithms and machine learning models to analyze market data and identify profitable trading opportunities. By incorporating AI into your trading strategies, you can automate the process of analyzing vast amounts of data and making trading decisions based on predefined rules and parameters.

One of the key advantages of algorithmic trading strategies with AI is their ability to adapt to changing market conditions in real-time. AI-powered trading bots can quickly adjust to new information and market trends, allowing you to capitalize on opportunities as they arise and minimize potential losses.

To successfully implement algorithmic trading strategies with AI, it is important to have a solid understanding of both the underlying technology and the principles of trading options. By combining your knowledge of AI with your expertise in options trading, you can create a powerful trading bot that can execute trades with speed and precision.

In the upcoming sections, we will delve deep into a wide range of highly sought-after algorithmic trading strategies that harness the power of AI technology. We will also share valuable insights on seamlessly incorporating AI-driven trading bots into your options trading portfolio, offering you a competitive edge in the market. By honing your skills in algorithmic trading with AI, you have the chance to significantly boost your trading performance and achieve unparalleled success in the fiercely competitive realm of stock and options trading. Through dedication and strategic execution, the potential for growth and profitability is boundless, opening up a world of opportunities for you to explore and capitalize on.

Chapter 36. AI-Based Risk Assessment in Options Trading

Chapter 36: AI-Based Risk Assessment in Options Trading

In the world of options trading, risk assessment is a crucial component of making informed decisions. With the advancements in artificial intelligence (AI) technology, traders now have access to powerful tools that can help them assess and manage risk more effectively. This subchapter will explore how AI-based risk assessment can be utilized in options trading to improve trading outcomes.

One of the key benefits of using AI in risk assessment is its ability to analyze vast amounts of data quickly and accurately. AI algorithms can process market data, historical trends, and other relevant information to identify potential risks and opportunities in real-time. By leveraging this technology, traders can make more informed decisions based on data-driven insights rather than relying solely on intuition.

AI-powered trading bots are increasingly being used to execute options trades based on predefined risk parameters. These bots can continuously monitor market conditions and adjust trading strategies accordingly to minimize risk exposure. By incorporating AI-based risk assessment into their trading practices, traders can potentially increase their chances of success while minimizing losses.

Furthermore, AI can help traders identify patterns and trends that may not be immediately apparent to the human eye. By analyzing historical data and market behavior, AI algorithms can uncover potential risks that traders may have overlooked. This can be especially useful for novice traders who are still learning the ropes of options trading and may not have the experience to identify risks on their own.

Overall, AI-based risk assessment in options trading has the potential to revolutionize the way traders approach risk management. By harnessing the power of AI technology, traders can gain a competitive edge in the market and make more informed decisions that are backed by data-driven insights. For those who are eager to learn more about trading stocks and options, mastering AI-powered trading bots for executing options trades can be a valuable skill to have in today's fast-paced and dynamic market environment.

Chapter 37. Natural Language Generation for Trading Reports

In Chapter 37 of "Mastering AI-Powered Trading Bots for Options," we delve into the fascinating world of Natural Language Generation (NLG) for trading reports. NLG is a branch of artificial intelligence (AI) that focuses on the automatic generation of human-like text from data. This technology has revolutionized the way trading reports are created, making them more insightful and easier to understand for traders of all levels.

For those of you who are just starting out in the world of trading stocks and options, understanding how NLG can be used to create trading reports is essential. With the help of AI-powered trading bots, you can now generate comprehensive reports that provide valuable insights into market trends, trading strategies, and potential risks. By leveraging NLG technology, you can make more informed decisions when it comes to executing options trades.

One of the key benefits of using NLG for trading reports is the ability to customize the content to suit your specific needs. Whether you are a novice trader looking for basic information or an experienced investor seeking in-depth analysis, NLG can tailor the reports to meet your requirements. This level of customization ensures that you receive the most relevant and actionable insights to help you make profitable trades in the options market.

Furthermore, NLG can also help you stay up-to-date with the latest market developments and trends. By automatically generating reports based on real-time data, AI-powered trading bots can provide you with timely information that can give you a competitive edge in the fast-paced world of options trading. This proactive approach to market analysis can help you identify opportunities and mitigate risks before they impact your trading portfolio.

In conclusion, mastering the use of NLG for trading reports is a valuable skill for anyone looking to excel in the world of AI-powered trading bots for options. By understanding how to leverage this technology effectively, you can enhance your decision-making process, improve your trading strategies, and ultimately increase your chances of success in the dynamic and ever-evolving options market. So, embrace the power of NLG and take your trading game to the next level!

Chapter 38. AI and Market Anomalies

In Chapter 38 of "Mastering AI-Powered Trading Bots for Options," we delve into the fascinating intersection of AI and market anomalies. As individuals eager to learn about trading stocks and options, understanding how AI can identify and capitalize on market anomalies is crucial for success in the world of trading. Market anomalies refer to the deviations from the efficient market hypothesis, where prices do not reflect all available information. AI-powered trading bots have the ability to spot these anomalies and exploit them for profit.

One of the key benefits of using AI in trading options is its ability to analyze vast amounts of data in real-time to identify patterns and anomalies that human traders may overlook. By leveraging machine learning algorithms, AI-powered trading bots can detect subtle changes in market behavior and make informed trading decisions accordingly. This gives traders a competitive edge in capitalizing on market inefficiencies and maximizing their returns.

AI-powered trading bots are particularly effective in identifying anomalies in options markets, where complex pricing models and strategies can lead to mispricings and arbitrage opportunities. By continuously monitoring market data and executing trades based on predefined criteria, these bots can take advantage of temporary discrepancies in options pricing to generate profits. This automated approach eliminates human emotions and biases, allowing for more consistent and disciplined trading strategies.

In Chapter 38, we explore the various types of market anomalies that AI-powered trading bots can detect, such as pricing anomalies, volume anomalies, and event-driven anomalies. By understanding how these anomalies can impact options pricing and trading strategies, individuals can develop more effective trading algorithms and improve their overall performance in the market. With the right tools and knowledge, traders can leverage AI to navigate the complexities of the options market and achieve their financial goals.

In conclusion, Chapter 38 provides valuable insights into the role of AI in identifying and exploiting market anomalies in the world of options trading. By learning how AI-powered trading bots can analyze market data and make informed decisions, individuals can enhance their trading strategies and increase their chances of success in the market. With a solid understanding of AI and market anomalies, traders can harness the power of technology to optimize their trading performance and achieve their desired outcomes.

Chapter 39. Sentiment Analysis in Volatility Trading

Chapter 39: Sentiment Analysis in Volatility Trading

In the world of trading stocks and options, understanding market sentiment is crucial for making informed decisions. Sentiment analysis involves analyzing the emotions and opinions of market participants to gauge the overall market mood. This can be especially useful in volatility trading, where market sentiment can have a significant impact on price movements.

One way to incorporate sentiment analysis into your trading strategy is through the use of AI-powered trading bots. These bots can analyze large amounts of data from various sources, such as news articles, social media, and financial reports, to identify trends and patterns that may indicate shifts in market sentiment. By leveraging AI technology, traders can gain valuable insights into market sentiment and make more informed trading decisions.

When it comes to volatility trading, sentiment analysis can help traders anticipate potential market movements and adjust their positions accordingly. For example, if sentiment analysis indicates that market participants are feeling optimistic about a particular stock, this may lead to increased buying activity and a potential increase in volatility. By being aware of these shifts in sentiment, traders can capitalize on opportunities to profit from price fluctuations.

Furthermore, AI-powered trading bots can automate the process of sentiment analysis, allowing traders to react quickly to changing market conditions. These bots can continuously monitor market sentiment in real-time and execute trades based on predefined criteria. This not only saves time and effort for traders but also ensures that trades are executed at the most opportune moments.

In conclusion, incorporating sentiment analysis into volatility trading can be a powerful tool for traders looking to enhance their trading strategy. By leveraging AI-powered trading bots to analyze market sentiment, traders can gain valuable insights into market trends and make more informed decisions. With the right tools and technology, traders can navigate the complexities of volatility trading with confidence and precision. Additionally, utilizing sentiment analysis can help traders better understand market psychology and make more strategic decisions based on the collective emotions of market participants. By staying ahead of market sentiment trends, traders can adapt their strategies more effectively and capitalize on opportunities that may arise in volatile market conditions. Ultimately, integrating sentiment analysis into volatility trading can provide traders with a competitive edge and improve their overall trading performance.

Chapter 40. Machine Learning for Risk Prediction in Options Trading

In the world of trading stocks and options, the use of machine learning for risk prediction has become increasingly popular. By harnessing the power of artificial intelligence, traders can make more informed decisions when it comes to executing options trades. In this chapter, we will explore the role of machine learning in risk prediction and how it can be used to improve your trading strategies.

Machine learning algorithms can analyze vast amounts of data and identify patterns that may not be immediately apparent to human traders. By using historical market data, these algorithms can predict the likelihood of certain events occurring in the future, such as price movements or market volatility. This information can then be used to make more accurate predictions about the risks associated with different options trades.

One of the key benefits of using machine learning for risk prediction in options trading is the ability to automate the decision-making process. AI-powered trading bots can be programmed to continuously monitor market conditions and adjust trading strategies accordingly. This not only saves time and effort for traders but also ensures that decisions are based on data-driven insights rather than emotions or gut feelings.

Furthermore, machine learning algorithms can help traders identify potential risks and opportunities that may not be immediately obvious. By analyzing data from multiple sources, these algorithms can uncover hidden patterns and correlations that can inform trading strategies. This can give traders a competitive edge in the market and help them make more informed decisions about when to enter or exit trades.

Overall, mastering AI-powered trading bots for options can greatly enhance your trading capabilities and improve your overall profitability. By utilizing machine learning for risk prediction, traders can make more informed decisions, reduce their exposure to risk, and increase their chances of success in the market. So, if you are eager to learn more about AI and trading options, this chapter is a great place to start your journey towards becoming a successful options trader.

Chapter 41. Quantum Computing and Options Trading

Chapter 41: Quantum Computing and Options Trading

In this chapter, we will explore the exciting intersection of quantum computing and options trading. Quantum computing is a cutting-edge technology that has the potential to revolutionize many industries, including finance. As people who are eager to learn about trading stocks and options, it is essential to understand how quantum computing can impact the world of options trading.

Quantum computing offers the potential to solve complex problems at speeds that are unimaginable with classical computers. This increased computational power opens up new possibilities for options traders, allowing them to analyze vast amounts of data and make more informed trading decisions. By leveraging quantum computing, traders can gain a competitive edge in the options market and potentially increase their profits.

One of the key advantages of quantum computing in options trading is its ability to perform complex calculations and simulations in a fraction of the time it would take a traditional computer. This speed allows traders to quickly analyze market trends, assess risk, and execute trades with precision. By incorporating quantum computing into their trading strategies, traders can react more swiftly to market fluctuations and capitalize on profitable opportunities.

As we delve deeper into the world of AI and options trading, it is important to consider the potential impact of quantum computing on the development of AI-powered trading bots. These bots rely on advanced algorithms and machine learning techniques to execute trades on behalf of traders. By integrating quantum computing into the design of these bots, developers can create more sophisticated and efficient trading algorithms that can adapt to changing market conditions in real-time.

In conclusion, the intersection of quantum computing and options trading represents a compelling opportunity for those looking to enhance their trading skills. By understanding how quantum computing can improve the speed and accuracy of options trading, traders can position themselves for success in the ever-evolving financial markets. As you continue your journey to mastering AI-powered trading bots for options, consider the potential benefits of incorporating quantum computing into your trading strategies.

Chapter 42. AI-Driven Trading Algorithms

Chapter 42: AI-Driven Trading Algorithms

In this chapter, we will delve into the fascinating world of AI-driven trading algorithms and how they are revolutionizing the way we trade stocks and options. As technology continues to advance at a rapid pace, artificial intelligence has emerged as a powerful tool for analyzing market data and making informed trading decisions. For those who are just beginning to learn about trading stocks and options, understanding how AI-driven algorithms work can provide a valuable edge in the market.

AI-driven trading algorithms utilize complex mathematical models and algorithms to analyze vast amounts of market data in real-time. These algorithms can quickly identify trading opportunities and execute trades with precision and speed that is unmatched by human traders. By leveraging AI technology, traders can take advantage of market inefficiencies and make more profitable trades.

One of the key benefits of using AI-driven trading algorithms is their ability to adapt to changing market conditions. These algorithms can continuously learn and improve their performance over time, making them incredibly valuable tools for traders looking to stay ahead of the curve. By incorporating AI technology into their trading strategies, traders can increase their chances of success and achieve better results in the market.

For those interested in incorporating AI-powered trading bots into their options trading strategies, it is important to understand how these algorithms work and how to effectively use them to execute trades. By learning how to leverage AI technology in your trading, you can gain a competitive edge in the market and improve your overall trading performance. With the right knowledge and tools, anyone can become a successful trader in the world of options trading.

In conclusion, AI-driven trading algorithms are revolutionizing the way we trade stocks and options, offering traders a powerful tool for analyzing market data and making informed trading decisions. By understanding how these algorithms work and how to effectively use them in your trading strategies, you can increase your chances of success in the market. Whether you are a beginner or experienced trader, learning how to leverage AI technology in your trading can help you achieve better results and take your trading to the next level.

Chapter 43. Regulatory Compliance in AI Trading

In Chapter 43 of "Mastering AI-Powered Trading Bots for Options," we delve into the crucial topic of regulatory compliance in AI trading. As you begin your journey into the world of trading stocks and options, it is essential to understand the rules and regulations that govern the use of AI in trading. This subchapter will provide you with a comprehensive overview of the regulatory landscape and how it impacts AI-powered trading bots for executing options trades.

Regulatory compliance is a key consideration for anyone looking to engage in AI trading, as failure to adhere to the rules can result in serious consequences. In the United States, the Securities and Exchange Commission (SEC) plays a central role in regulating the use of AI in trading. It is important to familiarize yourself with the SEC's guidelines and requirements to ensure that your trading activities are in compliance with the law.

One of the primary concerns in AI trading is the potential for market manipulation. The use of AI-powered trading bots can create opportunities for traders to engage in manipulative practices that can harm the integrity of the market. As such, regulators are keen to ensure that AI traders are not engaging in any activities that could be considered manipulative or fraudulent.

In addition to market manipulation, regulators are also concerned about the potential for AI trading to exacerbate market volatility. The use of AI-powered trading bots can lead to rapid and unpredictable trading activity, which can have a destabilizing effect on the market. It is important for traders to be aware of these risks and to take steps to mitigate them through responsible trading practices.

By understanding the regulatory landscape and taking steps to ensure compliance, you can navigate the world of AI-powered trading bots with confidence. This subchapter will equip you with the knowledge and tools you need to trade options successfully while adhering to the rules and regulations that govern the use of AI in trading. With a solid understanding of regulatory compliance, you can trade with peace of mind and focus on achieving your financial goals.

Chapter 44. AI and Market Manipulation Detection

Chapter 44: AI and Market Manipulation Detection

In the world of trading stocks and options, the use of artificial intelligence (AI) has become increasingly prevalent. AI-powered trading bots have revolutionized the way trades are executed, making them faster and more efficient than ever before. One important aspect of utilizing AI in trading is the detection of market manipulation. Market manipulation refers to the illegal activity of artificially inflating or deflating the price of a security, which can have a significant impact on market stability and investor confidence.

AI can be a powerful tool in detecting market manipulation due to its ability to analyze vast amounts of data in real-time. By using advanced algorithms and machine learning techniques, AI-powered trading bots can identify patterns and anomalies in trading activity that may indicate market manipulation. This can help traders and investors make more informed decisions and protect themselves from potential risks.

One key advantage of using AI for market manipulation detection is its ability to process and analyze data at a speed and scale that is impossible for humans to achieve. This allows AI-powered trading bots to detect manipulative behavior quickly and accurately, giving traders a competitive edge in the market. By leveraging AI technology, traders can stay ahead of potential market manipulation schemes and protect their investments.

In addition to detecting market manipulation, AI can also help traders identify trading opportunities and execute trades more efficiently. By using AI-powered trading bots, traders can automate the process of analyzing market data, identifying trends, and executing trades based on predefined criteria. This can help traders make better decisions and maximize their profits while minimizing risks.

Overall, the integration of AI technology in trading options has the potential to revolutionize the way trades are executed and monitored. By utilizing AI-powered trading bots for market manipulation detection, traders can stay ahead of potential risks and make more informed decisions. As AI continues to evolve and improve, it will play an increasingly important role in the world of trading options, providing traders with new opportunities to succeed in the market.

Chapter 45. Fintech Innovations in Options Trading

Chapter 45: Fintech Innovations in Options Trading

In recent years, the world of options trading has experienced a revolution with the emergence of fintech innovations. These advancements have made it easier than ever for individuals to participate in the options market, even for those who are new to trading. From AI-powered algorithms to sophisticated trading bots, there are now more tools available to help traders navigate the complexities of options trading.

One of the most exciting developments in the world of options trading is the integration of artificial intelligence (AI) technology. AI-powered algorithms are able to analyze vast amounts of data in real-time, helping traders to make more informed decisions and execute trades with greater precision. By harnessing the power of AI, traders can gain a competitive edge in the market and increase their chances of success.

Another key innovation in options trading is the development of AI-powered trading bots. These bots are designed to automatically execute trades based on predefined parameters set by the trader. By using trading bots, individuals can take advantage of opportunities in the market without having to monitor their positions constantly. This can be especially beneficial for those who have limited time to devote to trading or who are new to the world of options.

For those who are new to trading stocks and options, learning how to harness the power of AI and trading bots can be a game-changer. By leveraging these technologies, individuals can streamline their trading process, reduce the risk of human error, and increase their chances of success in the market. With the right tools and knowledge, anyone can become a successful options trader and take advantage of the opportunities presented by fintech innovations.

In conclusion, fintech innovations in options trading have opened up new possibilities for individuals looking to enter the world of trading. By embracing AI-powered technology and trading bots, traders can gain a competitive edge in the market and increase their chances of success. For those who are eager to learn more about trading stocks and options, mastering the use of AI-powered trading bots can be a valuable skill that sets them apart in the world of options trading.

Chapter 46. AI and Market Forecasting

Chapter 46: AI and Market Forecasting

In this chapter, we will delve into the fascinating world of AI and market forecasting. For those of you who are just beginning to learn about trading stocks and options, understanding how artificial intelligence can be used to predict market trends can be a game-changer in your trading strategy. By harnessing the power of AI, traders can make more informed decisions and potentially increase their chances of success in the market.

AI and trading options go hand in hand when it comes to market forecasting. AI-powered trading bots are revolutionizing the way traders execute options trades by analyzing vast amounts of data and identifying patterns that human traders may overlook. These bots can help traders make more accurate predictions about market movements, leading to potentially higher profits and lower risks.

One of the key benefits of using AI for market forecasting is its ability to process and analyze data at a speed and scale that is simply not possible for humans. By leveraging machine learning algorithms, AI-powered trading bots can quickly adapt to changing market conditions and make real-time decisions based on the most up-to-date information available. This can give traders a significant edge in the market and help them stay ahead of the curve.

When it comes to AI and market forecasting, it is essential to understand that while AI can provide valuable insights and predictions, it is not infallible. Market conditions can change rapidly, and there are always unforeseen variables that can impact the accuracy of AI-generated forecasts. It is important for traders to use AI as a tool to supplement their own knowledge and experience, rather than relying solely on AI-powered trading bots for all their trading decisions.

In conclusion, mastering the use of AI for market forecasting can be a powerful tool for traders looking to improve their trading strategies and increase their chances of success in the market. By understanding how AI-powered trading bots can help predict market trends and make informed decisions, traders can take their trading to the next level and potentially achieve greater profits in the world of options trading.

Chapter 47. AI Ethics and Bias in Trading

In the fast-paced world of trading stocks and options, the use of artificial intelligence (AI) has become increasingly prevalent. AI-powered trading bots have revolutionized the way trades are executed, allowing for faster and more efficient decision-making processes. However, with this advancement comes the potential for ethical concerns and biases in trading.

When it comes to AI ethics in trading, it is essential for traders to be aware of the potential implications of using AI-powered trading bots. One major concern is the possibility of bias in the algorithms used to make trading decisions. Bias can occur when the data used to train the AI models is not representative of the broader market, leading to skewed results and potentially harmful outcomes for traders.

To address this issue, traders must ensure that the data used to train AI-powered trading bots is diverse and inclusive, representing a wide range of market conditions and scenarios. Additionally, traders should regularly monitor the performance of their AI models and adjust them as needed to minimize bias and ensure fair and ethical trading practices.

In addition to bias, traders must also consider the ethical implications of using AI-powered trading bots. Ethical concerns may arise when AI algorithms are used to make decisions that impact market outcomes and potentially harm other traders or investors. It is crucial for traders to establish clear guidelines and principles for using AI in trading to ensure that their actions are ethical and in line with industry standards.

Overall, mastering AI-powered trading bots for options requires a deep understanding of AI ethics and bias in trading. By being mindful of potential biases in AI algorithms and making ethical decisions when using AI in trading, traders can navigate the complexities of the market with confidence and integrity. With the right approach, AI-powered trading bots can be powerful tools for executing options trades responsibly and ethically.

Chapter 48. AI-Based Market Surveillance

In Chapter 48 of "Mastering AI-Powered Trading Bots for Options," we delve into the fascinating world of AI-based market surveillance. For those who are just beginning to learn about trading stocks and options, understanding how artificial intelligence can be used to monitor and analyze market activity is crucial for making informed trading decisions.

AI-based market surveillance involves using advanced algorithms and machine learning techniques to track and analyze market data in real-time. These AI-powered systems are capable of processing vast amounts of information quickly and accurately, allowing traders to identify patterns, trends, and anomalies that may impact the market.

By harnessing the power of AI for market surveillance, traders can stay ahead of the curve and make more informed decisions when it comes to executing options trades. AI can help traders identify potential opportunities and risks, as well as detect market manipulation and other fraudulent activities.

One of the key benefits of AI-based market surveillance is its ability to automate the monitoring process, freeing up traders to focus on strategy development and execution. By using AI-powered trading bots to execute options trades based on market surveillance data, traders can take advantage of opportunities in the market more efficiently and effectively.

Overall, AI-based market surveillance is a powerful tool for traders looking to stay competitive in the fast-paced world of options trading. By leveraging the capabilities of AI-powered systems to monitor market activity, traders can make better-informed decisions and maximize their profitability. So, if you're interested in AI and trading options, mastering AI-based market surveillance is essential for success in today's dynamic market environment.

Chapter 49. Deep Reinforcement Learning in Options Trading

In Chapter 49 of "Mastering AI-Powered Trading Bots for Options," we delve into the exciting world of deep reinforcement learning in options trading. This advanced technique combines the power of artificial intelligence with the complexities of trading options to create a dynamic and efficient trading strategy. For those eager to learn about trading stocks and options, understanding deep reinforcement learning can provide a competitive edge in the market.

Deep reinforcement learning is a subset of machine learning that focuses on teaching an AI agent how to make decisions through trial and error. By rewarding the agent for making profitable trades and penalizing it for losses, the AI is able to learn optimal trading strategies over time. In the context of options trading, deep reinforcement learning can be used to identify patterns in market data, predict price movements, and execute trades with precision.

One of the key benefits of using deep reinforcement learning in options trading is its ability to adapt to changing market conditions. Traditional trading strategies may become less effective as market dynamics shift, but an AI-powered trading bot utilizing deep reinforcement learning can quickly adjust its approach to maximize profits and minimize risks. By continuously learning and evolving, these bots can stay ahead of the curve in the fast-paced world of options trading.

For those new to the world of AI and trading options, it's important to understand the potential risks and rewards associated with deep reinforcement learning. While this advanced technique can offer significant advantages in terms of efficiency and profitability, it also requires a solid understanding of market dynamics and a willingness to take calculated risks. By combining AI-powered trading bots with deep reinforcement learning, traders can unlock new opportunities for success in the options market.

In conclusion, Chapter 49 of "Mastering AI-Powered Trading Bots for Options" provides a comprehensive overview of deep reinforcement learning in options trading. By leveraging the power of artificial intelligence and advanced machine learning techniques, traders can enhance their ability to analyze market data, predict price movements, and execute profitable trades. For those looking to expand their knowledge and skills in the niche of AI and trading options, deep reinforcement learning offers a valuable tool for achieving success in the competitive world of options trading.

Chapter 50. The Intersection of AI and Behavioral Economics in Options Trading

In Chapter 50 of our book, "Mastering AI-Powered Trading Bots for Options," we delve into the fascinating intersection of artificial intelligence (AI) and behavioral economics in options trading. This subchapter focuses on how these two disciplines come together to inform trading decisions and strategies in the dynamic world of financial markets. For those who are eager to learn about trading stocks and options, understanding how AI and behavioral economics play a role in options trading is crucial for success.

AI has revolutionized the way trades are executed in the financial markets, and options trading is no exception. By utilizing advanced algorithms and machine learning techniques, AI-powered trading bots can analyze vast amounts of data to identify trading opportunities and make informed decisions in real-time. This can help traders take advantage of market trends and fluctuations with greater speed and accuracy than ever before.

Behavioral economics, on the other hand, focuses on how psychological and emotional factors influence decision-making in financial markets. By understanding human behavior and biases, traders can better anticipate market movements and adjust their strategies accordingly. When combined with AI, behavioral economics can provide valuable insights into market sentiment and help traders make more rational and profitable trading decisions.

One of the key benefits of leveraging AI and behavioral economics in options trading is the ability to automate trading processes and reduce the impact of human error. AI-powered trading bots can execute trades based on predefined criteria and parameters, eliminating the need for manual intervention and reducing the risk of emotional bias. By incorporating insights from behavioral economics, traders can further refine their strategies and improve their overall trading performance.

Overall, the intersection of AI and behavioral economics in options trading offers a wealth of opportunities for traders looking to enhance their skills and maximize their profits. By understanding how these disciplines work together to inform trading decisions, traders can gain a competitive edge in the fast-paced world of financial markets. Whether you are new to trading stocks and options or looking to take your skills to the next level, mastering AI-powered trading bots for executing options trades can help you achieve your goals and succeed in the market.

Conclusion

Recap of Key Concepts

In this subchapter, we will recap some of the key concepts we have covered so far in our journey to mastering AI-powered trading bots for options. For those of you who are new to trading stocks and options, this recap will help reinforce your understanding of the important principles and strategies that are essential for success in this field.

First and foremost, it is crucial to understand the basics of options trading. Options are financial derivatives that give investors the right, but not the obligation, to buy or sell an underlying asset at a specified price within a certain time frame. There are two types of options: call options, which give the holder the right to buy the underlying asset, and put options, which give the holder the right to sell the underlying asset.

Next, we explored the role of artificial intelligence (AI) in trading options. AI-powered trading bots use complex algorithms to analyze market data, identify patterns, and execute trades automatically. These bots can help traders make faster and more informed decisions, leading to potentially higher profits and reduced risk.

One key concept to understand when using AI-powered trading bots for executing options trades is risk management. It is important to set stop-loss orders and implement proper risk-reward ratios to protect your capital and minimize losses. Additionally, diversifying your options portfolio and using proper position sizing can help spread risk and optimize returns.

Another important concept covered in this subchapter is backtesting. Backtesting involves running historical data through a trading strategy to see how it would have performed in the past. This helps traders evaluate the effectiveness of their strategies and make necessary adjustments to improve performance in real-time trading.

In conclusion, mastering AI-powered trading bots for options requires a solid understanding of options trading basics, the role of AI in trading, risk management strategies, backtesting, and continuous learning and adaptation. By applying these key concepts, you can enhance your trading skills and increase your chances of success in the dynamic world of options trading.

Tips for Continued Learning and Improvement

As you continue your journey into the world of trading stocks and options, it is important to focus on continued learning and improvement. The field of AI-powered trading bots for executing options trades is constantly evolving, and staying up-to-date with the latest trends and techniques is essential for success. In this subchapter, we will discuss some tips for how you can continue to improve your skills and knowledge in this exciting and dynamic field.

First and foremost, never stop learning. There are countless resources available to help you expand your knowledge of AI and trading options, including online courses, webinars, books, and seminars. Take advantage of these resources to stay informed about the latest developments in the industry and to learn new strategies for optimizing your trading bot's performance.

Additionally, consider joining a trading community or forum where you can connect with other traders who share your interests and goals. These communities can be valuable sources of information and support, and can provide you with opportunities to network with other professionals in the field. By participating in these communities, you can gain insights from others' experiences and learn from their successes and failures.

Another important tip for continued learning and improvement is to practice, practice, practice. The more you use your AI-powered trading bot to execute options trades, the more comfortable and proficient you will become. Take the time to experiment with different strategies and techniques, and don't be afraid to make mistakes – they are an essential part of the learning process.

Lastly, don't be afraid to seek out feedback from others. Whether it's from a mentor, a fellow trader, or even your AI-powered trading bot itself, feedback can help you identify areas for improvement and make adjustments to your trading strategy. Embrace constructive criticism and use it as a tool for growth and development in your trading journey.

By following these tips for continued learning and improvement, you can enhance your skills and knowledge in the field of AI-powered trading bots for executing options trades. Remember that learning is a lifelong process, and by staying curious, open-minded, and dedicated to your craft, you can achieve success in this exciting and dynamic industry.

Final Thoughts on Mastering AI-Powered Trading Bots for Options

In conclusion, mastering AI-powered trading bots for options can be a game-changer for those looking to enhance their trading strategies in the stock market. By leveraging the power of artificial intelligence, traders can automate their trades, minimize emotions, and take advantage of market opportunities more efficiently. It is crucial for individuals who are eager to learn about trading stocks and options to understand the potential benefits and risks associated with using AI-powered bots in their trading activities.

One key takeaway from this subchapter is the importance of developing a solid understanding of how AI-powered trading bots work and how they can be used to execute options trades effectively. By grasping the fundamental concepts behind these bots, traders can make informed decisions and optimize their trading strategies for better outcomes. Additionally, staying informed about the latest advancements in AI technology and trading options is essential for those looking to stay ahead in the ever-evolving financial markets.

Furthermore, mastering AI-powered trading bots for options requires continuous learning and adaptation to market conditions. Traders must be willing to put in the time and effort to refine their strategies, analyze data, and make adjustments as needed. It is also crucial for individuals to stay disciplined and patient when using AI-powered bots, as impulsive decisions can lead to significant losses in the market.

Overall, the integration of AI technology into trading options presents exciting opportunities for individuals looking to enhance their trading skills and achieve better results in the stock market. By mastering AI-powered trading bots, traders can gain a competitive edge, automate repetitive tasks, and optimize their trading strategies for success. With dedication, persistence, and a willingness to learn, anyone can unlock the potential of AI-powered bots and take their trading to the next level.